The Moon And Her Flowers

A collective of Tanka, Haiku and Short Poetry

Brittany Strand

BookLeaf Publishing

India | USA | UK

Dedication

To everyone I have ever loved
and everyone I will ever come to love.
You have inspired me to become the person I am today
and the person I am tomorrow.

Preface

In the quiet corners of a simple heart
We follow a journey of love and sorrow
The Moon and Her Flowers
Highlights human connection
Through a series of short poetry

Acknowledgements

This book would not have been possible without the unwavering love and support of my friends and family.
You illuminate my life.
I thank each and every one of you for always believing in me.
A special thanks to my grandma for her continued love and support in my life, I wouldn't be here without you.
I know you'll always be my number one fan.
But I'll always be yours too, **I love you Grammy**.

The Girl

A simple *human*
And her heart, filled with *conflict*
She found herself *lost*
Pieces of her, *fragmented*
She was a *stained glass window*

Lost

The fire burns like the touch of your finger tips
    Where your hands were pressed against my skin
There's traces of you left on my lips
A dozen of your fingerprints
Left dancing on my skin
    Memories of you and I
Like dreams stuck in my mind
    I'm always thinking of your sonder brown eyes
And the way they look in soft golden light
    The air smells like your favorite cigarettes
And the honey scent of your soft kiss
    The taste of you lingers

I am ***lost***

Fragmented

The story of you...

The story of you is how I lost me..

When I met you I intended to spend the rest of my life
alone
    That was when you showed me home
Filling the empty spaces of my chest
    I was healing putting my weary bones to rest
A topsy turvey emptiness nonetheless
    I've grown a garden over those old weary bones
Growing I vowed never again to share the empty space
inside my head
    I had found me before I ever found you
However this isn't the story of me
    This is the story of you stardust boy with your
snake tattoos
How I stumbled about the door where you stood
    Though it's a door I never should have opened
Of course I did because there you stood with your
somber eyes and auburn brown hair
    Your hand stretched out from the darkness
Looking for light one that shined just like the sun
    Like a moth searching for flames

You looked at me in a way I had never seen
    I should've understood it could only mean one thing
Still I took your hand
    We coalesced in that dark room
In the cold emptiness
    We danced in the light of the moon
There I thought I love you
    Not knowing it's too soon
I was finding me before I ever found you
    Now I must start all over again
Let all the butterflies out of my cold now empty chest

I am **fragmented**

Human

I like to think that I have gentle hands
With gentle grasps
Soft and subtle
That when I hold you
You'll feel safe

    Do I have gentle hands?
    With safe spaces
    Where your fingers might land

I like to think that I have gentle hands
For my bones are a temple
Where-in stands a thousand walls
Lies, deception, and sorrow built them

    Do I have gentle hands?
    Ones that show who I truly am
    Where my bones become a soft place to land

I like to think that I have gentle hands
So I can carry the warmth of my heart in them
I'll never know if I have gentle hands
I cannot feel the warmth of my own skin

I am only *human*

Conflict

I once heard someone say something
    About the unfed mind
And something along the lines of how we devour
ourselves
    For the sake of staying stagnant
Like dusty books left sitting on library shelves
    A sepulcher of unread pages
Oh how we loved the stories the first time we read them
    Holding on to the past
Leaving no room for growth we become self destructive
    Knowing the feelings won't last
We must move forward
    Move on from the past
Life's always changing lest we forget
    He wasn't the first he won't be your last
Move on hunny it's for the best
    I know it hurts
But lay them to rest
The butterflies fluttering in your chest
Don't worry darling, about the thoughts in your head

You don't need this internal **conflict**

Stained Glass Window

My heart is a ***stained glass window***

Like the one I used to stare at in church service
    While I sat on the pew as a small child
A mosaic of beautifully broken pieces
    Where my light can shine through them and I
become a rainbow
With so many miraculous shapes and colors
    I've finally come to understand what it means
When your heart is a stained glass window
    You are a reflection of all that you have loved
Of the people that love you now
    And of the people you come to love tomorrow
A patchwork quilt made of leftover scraps
    Just like the one your grandma built with her bare
hands
I am a mosaic of colors
    A mosaic of laughs
I carry a stained glass heart in my hands
    And I am happy

The Boy

A lonely lost *soul*
Left looking for *connection*
His tapestry *heart*
He left hanging on her *walls*
Stretched upon *the house they built*

Heart

He used to say how heavy the burden is
    Of carrying a heart as full as his
The weight of memories he could never forget
    His love and his dreams sat wasting away within it
But his heart was empty
    Caverns and cacophonies
Hollow bones and memories of his broken homes
    His touch was deadly
I could never tell you why I let his hands touch me
    The way he pretends to be a soft place to rest
Now I'm lost in the catacombs of his chest
    Giving my life to save death

I am his hollow **heart**

Soul

Remember the last time you killed a spider?

I sure do it was a cold autumn one Sunday
afternoon
The spider sat in the corner of my bathroom
At the time I was afraid I had yet to understand
I grabbed my shoe and I raised my hands
The spider crept from the corner I was terrified
Until I saw the sad look in his eyes
I slowly crept closer
He outstretched his little hands
He stood so still
While out of fear I went in for the kill
He never moved, it's something I'll never
understand
I'll always remember the way he outstretched his hands
Since then
I've stopped killing spiders
Instead I save them I'm trying to make amends
Now we are friends
One lives in my room and I wave at him
I've come to understand what I never understood
About what love means
The complexity of the empathy of a spider

And his tiny little *soul*

Connection

I wish I could be counting stars with you
    Collecting constellations
Just you and me and the moon
    The dew on the grass
And soft spoken I love you's
    I want to hold your hand
Feel your kisses like butterflies on my lips
    I won't take those moments for granted
Can't you see the seeds you've planted
    Grow flowers on my skin
It's 11:11 I make a wish
    For you to be by my side again
Before my bones decompose
    And I become a reflection
Oh my love you are heaven

I'll always crave this ***Connection***

Walls

2:00 A.M.
    I woke up to bricks in our bed
Thoughts racing through my head
    Always overthinking I'm feeling frustrated
What did I do wrong to get so mistreated

2:00 P.M.
    It was thanksgiving day
You wouldn't get out of the way
    Your bones became a cage
And I became a bird who couldn't see

2:00 A.M
    I wake up again to bricks in our bed
No racing thoughts
    I feel empty instead
With a heavy weight on my chest

2:00 P.M
    It was our last day
I had to say goodbye
    To keep my heart safe

Those bricks built **walls**

The House They Built

I remember **the house they built**

 Beneath the warmth of the sun
They built that house together with love
    In the backyard they planted a garden
Under the light of the moon
    I remember when that was me and you
Sharing a soft embrace in the rain
    And dancing in our garden day after day
I remember kisses planted upon my skin
    For every little achievement
Just like you promised there would be
    The soft smiles we shared by the fire
In the house we built
    With calloused hands
I remember the ghosts we used to carry
    And the skeletons in our closet
The ones we left in that old one bedroom apartment
    Where the walls had eyes
That we couldn't see
And the pillows had ears
That listened to us all night while we talked in our sleep
    Until we built a home
To set ourselves free

The Love

Forgotten *story*
Her eyes were filled with *starlight*
A new *addiction*
His heart filled with *butterflies*
This love won't last forever

Story

We used to use our laughter to face the distance
    Smiling so hard we'd forget
The one thousand seven hundred and fifty miles between
us
    Just two simple humans
With nothing to lose
    Two yearning hearts in two separate places
We started as strangers
    But we set the stage
To grow together
    In the most beautiful way
We took it slow
    To let love grow
Look how far we've made it
    Tonight we'll share the same bed and blankets
Through our laughter we closed the distance
    Never again will there be one thousand seven
hundred and fifty miles between us

My love this is our **story**

Starlight

I told the stars about you
> And they burned a little brighter

I told the stars of my love for you
> They gave me a meteor shower

So I could have a million wishes
> When they passed by

They lit up the sky
> Hoping like I

To be lost in the night
> With you and the moon and her flowers

Oh sweet boy made of **starlight**

Addiction

You are the amber taste of honey on my lips
    And my favorite part of the morning
I can hear you in the background softly snoring
    I feel your kiss on the rim of my teacup
I'm hooked on you
    Our pillow talk whispers float around the room
The Soft spoken sounds
    Of Moans and I love you's
Seeping out of our bedroom
    As we dance
Mind and body we coalesce
    Baby

I think you've become my greatest **addiction**

Butterflies

I can hear wing beats in my chest
    A gentle tightness in my ribs
My body feels fuzzy
    Like I've been shocked by ten thousand volts of
electricity
I never could have imagined the intensity
    Of us
Or how often you'd make me blush
    You are a breath of fresh air in my lungs
I can feel the gentle tightness of my ribs again
    It's just as I thought

You give me **butterflies**

The Rain

Calm before the ***storm***
Two hearts filled with pure ***chaos***
The place they found ***home***

Storm

Did you know there are flowers in the arctic?

Somewhere so cold it seems unexpected
    But I think the earth grew them there with
intention
Arctic flowers become a testament
    To the human ability to withstand
The sorrow we hold in the palms of our hands
    Many of us carry hurricane hearts
Bolstering smiles on our faces
    When we choose to find love in the harshest of
places
We learn one simple lesson
    Together we are brave
We will withstand the rain

You are my calm in the **_storm_**

Chaos

I thought you were magic
    Like the real kind
Not just some silly magician
    Pulling rabbits out of his hat
I fell so hard for all of your lies
    For all the times you pretended to be nice
With you I shared life
    When I put my whole heart on the line
You stole my breath
    And made me forget who I am
I will never trust you again

You are pure **chaos**

home

We built a castle we called **home**

Our throne a queen sized bed
One we'd share at night when we'd rest
The walls were stacked pillows
We lined with blankets
This is my happy place
From humble beginnings
To a life fit for kings
Nothing to everything
I can't imagine where I'd be without you
My hand in your hand forever and always
One life to the next
Every home we share will be our castle
For you I promise
From one life to the next